EXAMINING ISSUES THROUGH
POLITICAL CARTOONS

The Death Penalty

Titles in the Examining Issues Through Political Cartoons series include:

Civil Rights
The Death Penalty
Euthanasia
The Nazis
Watergate

EXAMINING ISSUES THROUGH
POLITICAL CARTOONS

The Death Penalty

Edited by Laura K. Egendorf

Daniel Leone, *President*
Bonnie Szumski, *Publisher*
Scott Barbour, *Managing Editor*

GREENHAVEN PRESS
SAN DIEGO, CALIFORNIA

THOMSON

GALE

Detroit • New York • San Diego • San Francisco
Boston • New Haven, Conn. • Waterville, Maine
London • Munich

Library of Congress Cataloging-in-Publication Data

The death penalty / Laura K. Egendorf, book editor.
    p. cm. — (Examining issues through political cartoons)
Includes bibliographical references and index.
    ISBN 0-7377-1101-9 (pbk. : alk. paper)
    ISBN 0-7377-1102-7 (lib. bdg. : alk. paper)
    1. Capital punishment—Caricatures and cartoons.
I. Egendorf, Laura K., 1973–   . II. Series.

HV8694 .D384 2002
364.44—dc21

                                      2001055748

Cover photo: Callahan. © 1993 John Callahan.
Reprinted by permission of Levin Represents.

Contents

Foreword

Political cartoons, also called editorial cartoons, are drawings that do what editorials do with words—express an opinion about a newsworthy event or person. They typically appear in the opinion pages of newspapers, sometimes in support of that day's written editorial, but more often making their own comment on the day's events. Political cartoons first gained widespread popularity in Great Britain and the United States in the 1800s when engravings and other drawings skewering political figures were fashionable in illustrated newspapers and comic magazines. By the beginning of the 1900s, editorial cartoons were an established feature of daily newspapers. Today, they can be found throughout the globe in newspapers, magazines, and online publications and the Internet.

Art Wood, both a cartoonist and a collector of cartoons, writes in his book *Great Cartoonists and Their Art*:

> Day in and day out the cartoonist mirrors history; he reduces complex facts into understandable and artistic terminology. He is a political commentator and at the same time an artist.

The distillation of ideas into images is what makes political cartoons a valuable resource for studying social and historical topics. Editorial cartoons have a point to express. Analyzing them involves determining both what the cartoon's point is and how it was made.

Sometimes, the point made by the cartoon may be one that the reader disagrees with, or considers offensive. Such cartoons expose readers to new ideas and thereby challenge them to analyze and question their own opinions and assumptions. In some extreme cases, cartoons provide vivid examples of the thoughts that lie behind heinous acts; for example, the cartoons created by the Nazis illustrate the anti-Semitism that led to the mass persecution of Jews.

Examining controversial ideas is but one way the study of political cartoons can enhance and develop critical thinking skills. Another aspect to cartoons is that they can use symbols to make their point quickly. For example, in a cartoon in *Euthanasia*, Chuck Asay depicts supporters of a legal "right to die" by assisted suicide as vultures. Vultures are birds that eat dead and dying animals and are often a symbol of repulsive and cowardly predators who take advantage of those who have met misfortune or are vulnerable. The reader can infer that Asay is expressing his opposition to physician-assisted suicide by suggesting that its supporters are just as loathsome as vultures. Asay thus makes his point through a quick symbolic association.

An important part of critical thinking is examining ideas and arguments in their historical context. Political cartoonists (reasonably) assume that the typical reader of a newspaper's editorial page already has a basic knowledge of current issues and newsworthy people. Understanding and appreciating political cartoons often requires such knowledge, as well as a familiarity with common icons and symbolic figures (such as Uncle Sam's representing the United States). The need for contextual information becomes especially apparent in historical cartoons. For example, although most people know who Adolf Hitler is, a lack of familiarity with other German political figures of the 1930s may create difficulty in fully understanding cartoons about Nazi Germany made in that era.

Providing such contextual information is one important way that Greenhaven's Examining Issues Through Political Cartoons series seeks to make this unique and revealing resource conveniently accessible to students. Each volume presents a representative and diverse collection of political cartoons focusing on a particular current or historical topic. An introductory essay provides a general overview of the subject matter. Each cartoon is then presented with accompanying information including facts about the cartoonist and information and commentary on the cartoon itself. Finally, each volume contains additional informational resources, including listings of books, articles, and websites; an index; and (for historical topics) a chronology of events. Taken together, the contents of each anthology constitute an amusing and informative resource for students of historical and social topics.

Introduction

" If men were angels," wrote James Madison, "no government would be necessary." However, since neither men nor women are angels, governments establish and enforce laws and impose punishments when those laws are violated. The severest of all these punishments is the death penalty.

The Death Penalty in Ancient Civilization and Europe

The best way to describe the death penalty from the eighteenth century B.C., when it was written into Babylonian law in the Code of Hammurabi, until the eighteenth century A.D., is "cruel and usual punishment." It was "cruel" because the methods used included stoning, drowning, and beheading in Babylon; stoning and crucifixion in ancient Rome; and burning at the stake or being crushed under heavy stones in medieval Europe. However, none of these punishments could compare to drawing and quartering, which was applied to particularly unfortunate criminals in England between the thirteenth and nineteenth centuries. These doomed convicts were hanged, removed from the gallows while still conscious, disemboweled, beheaded, quartered, and then placed on public display.

The death penalty in earlier times was "usual" because it was applied to a number of crimes that would receive considerably milder penalties today. For example, the Code of Hammurabi prescribed the death penalty not only for murder and burglary but also for the fraudulent sale of beer. Numerous petty crimes in Greece were deemed capital under the legal code of the Dracon of Athens (hence the term "draconian punishment"). In England, executions took place so regularly that more than seventy thousand people were executed in the first half of the sixteenth century.

European attitudes toward the death penalty began to change during the Enlightenment, the eighteenth-century philosophical and literary movement that emphasized science, reason, and respect for humanity. One way to respect humanity, it was thought, was to abolish a government's power to kill its citizens. In 1764, Italian criminologist Cesare Beccaria published *Essay on Crimes and Punishments*, which argued against capital punishment. According to Beccaria, imprisonment is a more effective punishment than execution:

> There are many who can look upon death with intrepidity and firmness, some through fanaticism, and others through vanity, which attends us even to the grave; others from a desperate resolution, either to get rid of their misery, or cease to live: but fanaticism and vanity forsake the criminal in slavery, in chains and fetters, in an iron cage, and despair seems rather the beginning than the end of their misery. The mind, by collecting itself and uniting all its force, can, for a moment, repel assailing grief; but its most vigorous efforts are insufficient to resist perpetual wretchedness.

British philosopher Jeremy Bentham was another early capital punishment abolitionist. His efforts to reduce the number of crimes that carried the death penalty succeeded in bringing the number of capital crimes in England from 350 in 1789 to 4 by the middle of the 1800s.

The Death Penalty in America

The history of capital punishment in the United States is nearly as long as the history of the nation. The first execution in the American colonies occurred in Virginia in 1622, when Daniel Frank was put to death for theft. Theft was not the only capital crime in early America. Among the 150 crimes for which a colonist could face execution, most likely by hanging, were arson and witchcraft. The Salem witchcraft trials led to the hanging of twenty-five people in 1692 and 1693.

American use of the death penalty continued after the American Revolution. But as was the case in eighteenth- and nineteenth-century

Europe, a movement to abolish the death penalty began to take hold in the United States. Benjamin Rush, a doctor who had signed the Declaration of Independence, was a leading prison reformer and advocate for an end to capital punishment. His reforms led to the building of modern, professionally staffed penitentiaries. According to Harry Henderson in his introduction to *Capital Punishment*, "For the first time, confinement became a realistic alternative punishment for many crimes."

The anti–death penalty movement continued in earnest in the 1830s and 1840s. However, despite the efforts of men such as Walt Whitman and Horace Greeley, the abolitionists had little success. By the 1850s, only Michigan, Rhode Island, and Wisconsin had repealed their states' death penalty laws. The abolitionist movement was reborn in the early twentieth century during the Progressive Era and was somewhat more successful than it had been a half century earlier; by 1917, twelve states had banned capital punishment.

The abolitionist movement has continued in waves since then. As of 2001, thirty-eight states permit capital punishment. The death penalty is not used in Alaska, Hawaii, Iowa, Maine, Massachusetts, Michigan, Minnesota, North Dakota, Rhode Island, Vermont, West Virginia, Wisconsin, and the District of Columbia.

Supreme Court Decisions

Although abolitionist movements have had some impact on the death penalty in America, the U.S. Supreme Court has played the largest role in determining the acceptability of capital punishment. The Court's first important death penalty ruling was in 1879, in *Wilkerson v. Utah*. It decided that certain methods of execution could be considered "cruel and unusual," but did not rule whether the death penalty in general was a violation of the Eighth Amendment, which forbids the use of cruel and unusual punishment. Thirty-one years later, in *Weems v. United States*, the Court, in an opinion written by Justice Joseph McKenna, ruled that the definition of "cruel and unusual punishment" continually evolves, as public opinion becomes more enlightened. Since 1890, the methods of execution that have been deemed humane include the electric chair, the gas chamber, and lethal injection. Execution by firing squad is used on occasion in Idaho, Oklahoma, and Utah; Washington is the only state that allows a death row inmate to choose to die by hanging.

The most important Supreme Court decisions occurred in the 1970s. In 1972's *Furman v. Georgia*, the Court ruled that the death penalty was unconstitutional. In the Court's view, the death penalty violated the Eighth Amendment because it was applied capriciously and arbitrarily. For the next four years, no one was executed. Despite the temporary ban on executions, twenty-three states enacted new death penalty statutes between *Furman v. Georgia* and December 1973. In the 1976 case *Gregg v. Georgia*, the Supreme Court upheld the constitutionality of new death penalty statutes that had been written in Texas, Georgia, and Florida, effectively relegalizing capital punishment. Numerous decisions have followed in the past three decades, among them three key decisions in 1989: *Penry v. Lynaugh*, which stated that execution of the mentally retarded is not necessarily banned under the Eighth Amendment, and *Stanford v. Kentucky* and *Wilkins v. Missouri*, both of which held that prisoners who had committed a capital offense at the age of sixteen or seventeen could face the death penalty.

As these court decisions indicate, opinions on the death penalty continue to change. However, the arguments for and against capital punishment have remained the same throughout the years. Three of these arguments are whether the death penalty is just, whether it deters crime, and whether it is moral.

The Justice of the Death Penalty

A key argument in favor of the death penalty is that some crimes are so horrific, the only just and appropriate punishment is death. Advocates of capital punishment contend that—in opposition to the views of Beccaria and other abolitionists—imprisonment is not an adequate penalty. In an article in *National Review*, legal scholar Ernest van den Haag writes, "[There] are no fully satisfactory alternatives [to capital punishment]. Life imprisonment is not necessarily lifelong; life imprisonment without parole still allows governors to pardon prisoners."

However, critics of the death penalty question whether capital punishment can be considered just if it is not fairly applied. Many abolitionist groups claim that the death penalty affects minority defendants disproportionately. In its report "Rights for All: Killing with Prejudice," Amnesty International contends that many prosecutors exhibit bias when deciding to pursue the death penalty. For example, the organization found that as of 1998, only 15 of the 124 prisoners from Philadelphia on death row were white. In Houston County, Alabama, the district attorney sought the death penalty for twenty-two defendants, nineteen of whom were African American. The report also asserts that bias on the part of the police, judges, and jurors can lead to unfair application of the death penalty. Amnesty International concludes, "Beyond any reasonable doubt, the U.S. death penalty continues to reflect the deeply rooted prejudices of the society that condones its use. Amnesty International cannot find any evidence that current legal safeguards eliminate racial bias in the application of the death penalty." The Department of Justice, however, has refuted the findings of Amnesty International and other anti–death penalty organizations. A June 2001 report by the department stated, "[Capital] charges and submission to the review procedure for a decision about seeking the death penalty did not occur with any greater frequency in cases involving Black or Hispanic defendants than in cases involving White defendants." The department reported that in capital cases reviewed by the U.S. attorney general, the death penalty was sought for 38 percent of white defendants, 25 percent of black defendants, and 20 percent of Hispanic defendants.

The Question of Innocence

Race is not the only factor that might prevent a death penalty defendant from receiving a fair trial. Income can also affect a capital case. Poor defendants typically must rely on the counsel of public defenders. Although many of these lawyers are hardworking and represent their clients with vigor, stories abound about lawyers falling asleep during the trial, meeting their clients a day before the trial begins, and generally failing to present any arguments or evidence that might prevent a conviction and eventual death sentence. Inadequate representation sometimes results in innocent defendants being convicted. Although in some cases these errors are rectified while the prisoner waits on death row, the possibility of sentencing innocent people to death is one of the greatest controversies of the death penalty.

Hugo Bedau and Michael Radelet conducted the first major study of wrongful death penalty convictions. The report, "Miscarriages of Justice in Potentially Capital Cases," was published in the

Stanford Law Review in 1987. The two men, professors at Tufts University and the University of Florida, respectively, reviewed death penalty cases throughout the twentieth century and discovered that 350 prisoners who had been convicted of capital or potentially capital cases were later found innocent. Most of those defendants were pardoned or granted a retrial, but others were ultimately killed, most famously Nicola Sacco and Bartolomeo Vanzetti. Both were executed in 1927 for committing murder and armed robbery, despite the fact that another man confessed to the crime.

Other reports have followed Bedau and Radelet's seminal study. Alan Berlow, in an article for the *American Prospect*, reports that since 1973, ninety-six people have been freed from death row "either because they were proved innocent (ten of them on the basis of DNA) or because courts found unconscionable due-process violations." Among these prisoners was Anthony Porter, who was freed from Illinois's death row in 1999 when a Northwestern University journalism professor and five of his students proved that another man had committed the murders for which Porter had been convicted sixteen years earlier. Twelve other prisoners have been freed from Illinois's death row since 1977. In response, Illinois governor George Ryan instituted a moratorium on executions and established a commission to study why wrongful convictions occur. Interest in a similar moratorium at the national level is strong; according to a July 2000 poll, 63 percent of Americans believe a moratorium is needed to determine whether the death penalty is applied fairly.

However, not everyone is convinced that innocent defendants are convicted on a regular basis. Stephen Markman and Paul Cassell, who both served in the Department of Justice during the Reagan administration, analyzed the Bedau-Radelet report and concluded that sufficient evidence existed to prove the guilt of the purportedly innocent prisoners. Cassell also testified in front of Congress in 1993 on the issue of innocence. In his testimony, Cassell asserted,

The Bedau-Radelet article suffers from a number of flaws. To begin with, it uses a peculiar definition of "potentially capital" cases. The definition includes some allegedly erroneous rape executions, even though rape is no longer a capital offense under contemporary Supreme Court decisions. . . . The authors also have included a great number of cases from the early part of [the twentieth] century, long before the adoption of the extensive contemporary system of safeguards in the death penalty's administration, which greatly skews their analysis. Bedau and Radelet are able to identify only a very few "miscarriages of justice" in the decade since the Supreme Court upheld the constitutionality of the death penalty. Out of approximately 50,000 murder convictions during the period from 1977 to 1986, the authors point to only five cases where, they claim, a death penalty was wrongly imposed, and in none of these cases was the sentence actually carried out.

Death Qualification

In addition to concerns over wrongful convictions, people seeking to eliminate the death penalty often point out that the use of "death qualified juries" in capital cases decreases the chance that a defendant will receive life in prison if convicted. Death qualification is the procedure in which potential jurors who oppose the death penalty are barred from serving on a capital case. In 1968, the Supreme Court ruled that jurors could not be excluded if they merely had scruples against the death penalty. However, eighteen years later the Court stated that a prosecutor could excuse a juror who expressed any qualms about capital punishment. In 1992, the Court altered its opinion somewhat and ruled in *Morgan v. Illinois* that a juror who would always impose the death sentence may also be excused. Justice Byron White, in the majority opinion, explained why such jurors can prevent fair trials: "A juror who will automatically vote for the death penalty in every case will fail in good faith to consider the evidence of aggravating and mitigating circumstances as the instructions [in the Illinois death penalty statute] require him to do."

Despite the *Morgan* ruling, death penalty critics assert that people who oppose the death penalty are more likely than its proponents to be barred from serving on a capital case. A study by Howard University of forty-one capital cases revealed that 14.4 percent of jurors were excused for opposing the death penalty, compared to 0.5 percent for always favoring capital punishment. David Lindorff, writing for the online magazine *Salon*, refers to a 1994 study of California jury pools that revealed that, although minorities made up 18.5 percent of the pools, they represented 26.3 percent of those excluded from panels through the death-qualifying process. Lindorff contends that death qualification leads to juries that are largely white, male, and more likely to convict and to disregard the notion of presumption of innocence.

Capital Punishment and the Mentally Disabled

The final issue in the debate as to whether the death penalty is just is the treatment of mentally disabled defendants. Between 1976 and February 1997, at least thirty prisoners were executed despite showing signs of significantly below-average intelligence. For example, when Arkansas convict Rickey Ray Rector walked to the death chamber in 1992, he asked the guards to save the piece of pecan pie from his last meal so he could eat it later. Rector had been sentenced to death despite having the mind of a five-year-old. Arkansas is one of twenty-five states that permit the execution of mentally retarded defendants, which is typically defined as having an IQ under 70. Studies suggest that there may be as many as 250 such defendants on death row.

In his book *Dead Wrong: A Death Row Lawyer Speaks Out Against Capital Punishment*, Michael Mello offers several reasons why mentally retarded prisoners are at a particular disadvantage when trying to get their capital convictions overturned. According to Mello, "The mentally retarded prisoner . . . is unable to recall crucial details about events. His ability to communicate a complex chain of events prevents him from explaining to his attorney his role, if any, in crimes. . . . The ability of the mentally retarded defendant to present arguments is unquestionable."

Growing concern over the ethics of executing mentally retarded prisoners has led the Supreme Court to agree to reconsider whether it is constitutional to execute these defendants. The Court's ruling had not been made when this book went to press.

The Deterrence Effect of the Death Penalty

In addition to the view that capital punishment is the only just penalty for certain crimes, another argument in favor of the death penalty is that it deters crimes. Executions unquestionably serve as a "specific" deterrent—that is, they prevent a specific executed prisoner from commiting any further crimes. But executions can also purportedly serve as a "general" deterrent by disuading potential criminals from committing violent crimes out of fear of facing the death penalty.

According to death penalty advocates, the deterrence effect of the death penalty is significant. A 1985 study by University of North Carolina economist Stephen K. Layson found, that on average, eighteen murders are prevented per each execution. In an article for *National Review*, William Tucker observes that, although few people were executed in the early 1960s, the threat of capital punishment discouraged criminals from committing murder, thus steadily decreasing the homicide rate. However, he writes, "By 1966 there was a de facto moratorium in nearly all states, and in 1971 the Supreme Court overturned all existing death-penalty laws. But at zero executions, the predictable happened. Beginning in 1966, the rate of murder skyrocketed, soaring by 1980 to more than double the 1963 rate."

Opponents of capital punishment question the pro-deterrence argument. They point to the crime rates of states that do not use the death penalty, noting that those regions have less crime despite not executing their most violent perpetrators. For example, a survey in the *New York Times* found that, since 1980, states that permit capital punishment have had homicide rates 48 to 101 percent greater than states whose most severe penalty is life without parole. Critics also point to the lower crime rates in nations that have abolished capital punishment. Canada eliminated the death penalty in 1976. One year earlier, the homicide rate was 3.09 per 100,000 people. As of 1999, the rate was 1.76 per 100,000.

Perhaps surprisingly, people closely involved with the criminal justice system have expressed doubts about the death penalty's ability to deter crime. A survey of sixty-seven current and former presidents of the American Society of Criminology, the Academy of Criminal Justice Sciences, and the Law and Society Association found that over 80 percent believe there is no research that supports the deterrent effects of the death penalty. A 1995 poll of police chiefs in the United States revealed that two-thirds do not believe that the death penalty significantly reduces the number of homicides.

The deterrent effect of the death penalty on adolescents has also been debated. Since 1973, two hundred juveniles have been sentenced to death row. Of those prisoners, seventeen have been executed, including four in 2000. In a typical year, 2 to 3 percent of death sentences are imposed on defendants who were sixteen or seventeen when they committed their crimes, although these executions do not occur until after they have turned eighteen. For several reasons, the death penalty is considered an ineffective deterrent for adolescent criminals. The possibility of being executed for their crimes has little impact on youths growing up in violent neighborhoods and facing death on a daily basis. In addition, law professor Victor Streib notes that teenagers are impulsive and unable to plan ahead. According to Streib, "They think they are immortal, they don't fear death. Treating them like adults just assumes that they think like adults." Some death penalty experts suggest that long prison sentences are a more effective punishment for teenagers convicted of capital crimes.

The Death Penalty and Vengeance

The previous arguments are centered on the legal and social aspects of the death penalty. Yet the debate over capital punishment cannot be covered completely without considering the morality of the act. One of the most common criticisms of the death penalty is that the act is vengeful and immoral.

The leaders of many religious faiths have spoken out against the death penalty, asserting that it is wrong for a government to take the life of one of its citizens. One of these leaders, Pope John Paul II, stated his views on capital punishment in *Evangelium Vitae*. The pope declared,

> It is clear that . . . the nature and extent of the punishment must be carefully evaluated and decided upon, and ought not go to the extreme of executing the offender except in cases of absolute necessity: in other words, when it would not be possible otherwise to defend society. Today however, as a result of steady improvements in the organization of the penal system, such cases are very rare, if not practically non-existent.

> In any event, the principle set forth in the new Catechism of the Catholic Church remains valid: "If bloodless means are sufficient to defend human lives against an aggressor and to protect public order and the safety of persons, public authority must limit itself to such means, because they better

correspond to the concrete conditions of the common good and are more in conformity to the dignity of the human person."

However, other people argue that the death penalty is not vengeful or immoral; rather, it is the criminal acts that are an affront to humanity. Not all religions are abolitionist—Mormonism, Orthodox Judaism, and evangelistic Christianity are among the faiths that support the death penalty. In July 2000, the Southern Baptists adopted a pro–capital punishment resolution, declaring that God "established capital punishment as a just and appropriate means by which the civil magistrate may punish those guilty of capital crimes."

Secular writers also contend that governments have the right to execute certain criminals. Cathy Young, writing for *Reason*, observes, "If the government's monopoly on the use of force is legitimate, then, like it or not, the state may commit acts that would be criminal and immoral if committed by individuals." Columnist Jeff Jacoby asserts that the death penalty is moral because it is proportionate justice—murderers must pay for their acts with their own lives.

Cartoonists on the Death Penalty

The death penalty debate has not been expressed in words alone. Nearly every political cartoonist has depicted his or her views on the subject. In Examining Issues Through Political Cartoons: *The Death Penalty*, a variety of cartoonists consider capital punishment in the following chapters: The Morality of the Death Penalty, The Death Penalty as a Deterrent, The Fairness of the Death Penalty, and The Death Penalty and the Legal System. By examining these cartoons, it is hoped that the reader will develop a greater understanding of capital punishment and its place in American society.

Chapter 1

The Morality of the Death Penalty

Preface

Many supporters of the death penalty cite the Bible as proof that capital punishment is moral. They refer to passages that appear to indicate that a person who takes another's life should have his or her life taken in return. The most often cited of these passages are "an eye for an eye and a tooth for a tooth" and "Whoso sheddeth man's blood, by man shall his blood be shed: for in the image of God made he man." However, not every religious denomination considers the death penalty to be a morally acceptable punishment.

In general, the more conservative religions support capital punishment. In June 2000, the Southern Baptist Convention adopted a pro–death penalty resolution, stating that God "established capital punishment as a just and appropriate means by which the civil magistrate may punish those guilty of capital crimes." Columnist Jeff Jacoby explains the rationale for justifying the death penalty on religious grounds. He contends that the "eye for an eye" passage of the Bible is meant to instruct that the guilty must be punished in proportion to their crimes. According to Jacoby: "Exodus teaches a fundamental lesson about justice and decency: Criminal law must not permit vast disparities between the magnitude of the offense and the magnitude of the punishment. It is barbaric to hang pickpockets. . . . It is equally barbaric to turn murderers loose after six or seven years in prison." The more conservative and orthodox branches of Judaism also favor capital punishment.

However, not every conservative faith advocates the death penalty. Although conservative in its views on abortion and birth control, the Catholic Church has long opposed capital punishment. In his *Evangelium Vitae* (Gospel of Life), Pope John Paul II declared that capital punishment is permissible only "in cases of absolute necessity, in other words, when it would not be possible otherwise to defend society. Today, however, as a result of steady improvement in the organization of the penal system, such cases are very rare, if not practically nonexistent." Another Catholic criticism of the death penalty can be seen in the writings of Sister Helen Prejean, known for her work with prisoners on death row. Prejean disputes the views of Jacoby and others who believe in proportionate punishment. In an essay for the magazine *Salt of the Earth,* she writes: "I cannot believe in a God who metes out hurt for hurt, pain for pain, torture for torture. Nor do I believe that God invests human representatives with such power to torture and kill."

Among the more liberal denominations, the Quakers have long opposed the death penalty. In 1976 the faith adopted the position that capital punishment is immoral because of "the Quaker belief that every person has value in the eyes of God. . . . The death penalty restores no victim to life and only compounds the wrong committed in the first place." Other faiths that have stated their opposition to the death penalty include the Mennonites and the United Methodist Church. The Reform branch of Judaism has spoken out against capital punishment since the 1950s, when Ethel and Julius Rosenberg were executed after being convicted of espionage.

The morality of the death penalty is a constant source of debate. In the following chapter, the cartoonists depict several ethical arguments for and against capital punishment.

Examining Cartoon 1:

"It Doesn't Mean You're Allowed to Hit Him Back..."

About the Cartoon

One argument for the death penalty is that murder should be responded to with the ultimate punishment—the murderer must forfeit his or her own life. In this cartoon, Mickey Siporin ridicules this idea by depicting children making a similar argument about hitting, while their father—an off-duty executioner—points out the error in their thinking. In this way, Siporin suggests that the death penalty is inconsistent with the basic moral values society teaches its children.

About the Cartoonist

Mickey Siporin is a cartoonist whose works have appeared in the *Los Angeles Times*, the *New York Times*, and the *Village Voice*. He is also a filmmaker and a professor of cinematography and cartooning at Montclair State University in New Jersey.

Examining Cartoon 2:

"I'm Shocked at the Way Your Government Treats People . . ."

About the Cartoon

In this cartoon, Ben Sargent presents an ironic justification for America's use of the death penalty. He depicts a stereotypical American tourist who believes that the United States's use of the death penalty is preferable to the torture and abuse of prisoners in other nations' jails. Sargent suggests that America has a false sense of superiority and is in fact not much different from purportedly less civilized nations.

About the Cartoonist

Ben Sargent is the editorial cartoonist for the *Austin-American Statesman*. He won the 1982 Pulitzer Prize for editorial cartooning and is a former president of the Association of American Editorial Cartoonists. Sargent is also the author of *Texas Statehouse Blues* and *Big Brother Blues*.

Examining Cartoon 3:
"What Is Civilized . . ."

About the Cartoon

The death penalty is banned throughout Europe. However, euthanasia has been permitted in the Netherlands since 1973 and was formally legalized in 2000. Chip Bok's cartoon concerns the largely negative reaction President George W. Bush received during a trip to Europe in June 2001, during which his support for capital punishment was condemned. Bok criticizes what he sees as the hypocrisy in the European view, suggesting that in Europe the lives of criminals are protected while the elderly are discarded.

About the Cartoonist

Chip Bok, or Arthur B. Bok III, is the editorial cartoonist for Knight Ridder's *Akron Beacon Journal*. His cartoons appear in more than one hundred other publications including the *Washington Post*, the *New York Times*, *Newsweek*, and *Reason*. Among the first place awards he has garnered for his work are the 1995 National Cartoonist Society award for best editorial cartoonist, the 1993 Berryman Award given by the National Press Foundation for editorial cartoons, and the 1993 H.L. Mencken Award for editorial cartooning from the Free Press Association.

Examining Cartoon 4:

"Anything to Bring Back Civility to Our Society!"

About the Cartoon

Few executions have received as much attention as that of Timothy McVeigh, who was convicted in the April 19, 1995, bombing of the Murrah Federal Building in Oklahoma City, an act of terrorism that killed 168 people. His execution on June 11, 2001, received immense media attention. In this cartoon, drawn prior to the execution, David M. Hitch mocks the attitudes of those who want McVeigh to be put to death by depicting them as bloodthirsty.

This cartoon suggests that rather than being a civilizing influence, the death penalty is little more than an outlet for vengeance.

About the Cartoonist

David M. Hitch is the editorial cartoonist for the *Worcester Telegram and Gazette* in Massachusetts. In 1987 the National Newspaper Association presented him with its Best Original Cartoon award.

Examining Cartoon 5:

"Guess Whose Death Is Being Labeled 'Cruel'?"

PEDRO MEDINA: DIED INSTANTLY IN FLORIDA'S ELECTRIC CHAIR

DOROTHY JAMES: MEDINA'S VICTIM, DIED IN A POOL OF HER OWN BLOOD AN EXCRUCIATING 30 MINUTES AFTER BEING GAGGED AND STABBED 10 TIMES IN THE CHEST

Guess whose death is being labeled 'cruel'?

About the Cartoon

On March 24, 1997, Pedro Medina was executed at Florida State Prison for the murder of Dorothy James. At his execution, Medina was placed in an electric chair that had been built in 1924 and was nicknamed "Old Sparky." When the electricity was sent into Medina's body, foot-long flames shot out of his face and head for ten seconds, and the witnesses smelled burnt flesh. Following a year of controversy and debate, the Florida Supreme Court ruled that using the electric chair was not a violation of the constitutional ban on cruel and unusual punishment. In this cartoon, Mike Thompson asserts that the sympathy should be directed not toward Medina but toward his victim who suffered a vicious and fatal attack.

About the Cartoonist

Mike Thompson, an editorial cartoonist for the *Detroit Free Press*, previously worked for the *St. Louis Sun* and Copley Illinois newspapers. He has won the national H.L. Mencken Award for cartooning, the Charles M. Schulz Award, and the Association of American Editorial Cartoonists' Locher Award.

Examining Cartoon 6:

"Executing Women Will Send a Clear Message . . ."

About the Cartoon

In this cartoon Rob Rogers highlights the irony in the idea that the value of human life can be upheld by executing women and children who have committed murder. Rogers refers specifically to the execution of Karla Faye Tucker on February 3, 1998. Tucker, who was the first woman executed in Texas since the Civil War, had been sentenced to death for murdering two people with a pickax.

As the cartoon indicates, the United States does not permit the execution of children. However, of the thirty-eight states with the death penalty, twenty-three allow for the execution of convicted criminals who committed those crimes between the ages of sixteen and eighteen. Eighteen people have been executed for crimes they committed as juveniles since 1976.

About the Cartoonist

Rob Rogers has drawn editorial cartoons for the *Pittsburgh Post-Gazette* since 1993. His cartoons have also appeared in the *New York Times*, the *Washington Post*, *Newsweek*, and *U.S. News & World Report*. He was awarded the National Headliner Award in 1995.

Examining Cartoon 7:
"Revised Christian Coalition Edition"

About the Cartoon

In this cartoon, Chuck Asay comments on what he sees as the inconsistent views of Christians toward the death penalty. This cartoon refers specifically to the controversy surrounding the execution of Karla Faye Tucker on February 3, 1998, in Texas. While she was on death row, Tucker converted to Christianity and married the prison chaplain. Pat Robertson, founder and president of the Christian Coalition, a conservative religious organization, declared that Tucker had shown repentance and should not be executed. Robertson wrote: "She is totally transformed, and I think to execute her is more an act of vengeance than it is appropriate justice." Asay disagrees with Robertson's view and concludes that it is contrary to the tenets of the Bible to exempt a murderer from execution due to their religious conversion.

Robertson has since said that although he believes capital punishment is morally justified, a moratorium should be placed on the death penalty because it discriminates against African Americans and the poor.

About the Cartoonist

Chuck Asay is the editorial cartoonist for the *Colorado Springs Gazette* and is syndicated with Creators Syndicate in more than eighty newspapers nationwide. His collection of cartoons, *Asay Doodles Goes to Town,* was published in 1995.

Chapter 2

The Death Penalty as a Deterrent

Preface

For the death penalty to be an effective punishment, it should prevent people from committing murder and other capital crimes. Advocates and critics disagree about the deterrent effect of capital punishment.

Critics of the death penalty have observed that the states with the highest homicide rates are also the states in which the death sentence is most frequently imposed, suggesting that executions do not deter murderers. For example, the Bureau of Justice Statistics has reported that although 80 percent of all executions take place in the South, that region has the highest murder rate in the United States. In contrast, only 1 percent of all executions are held in the northeast region, but that area has the lowest murder rate. Since 1980, according to a survey in the *New York Times*, states with the death penalty have had homicide rates 48 percent to 101 percent higher than states that do not use capital punishment.

Death penalty foes also maintain that the experience of other nations shows that there is no deterrent effect to capital punishment. In its "Facts and Figures on the Death Penalty," Amnesty International details how abolishing the death penalty has affected Canada's murder rate. In 1975, the homicide rate in Canada was 3.09 per 100,000 population. Capital punishment was abolished the following year. By 1999, the rate had fallen 43 percent, to 1.76 per 100,000 population.

Death penalty supporters disagree with those findings, arguing that executing criminals deters other people from committing similar crimes. In a July 2000 opinion piece for the *National Review*, William Tucker writes: "The place where the death penalty clearly intercedes in a rational thought process is felony murder. This is murder committed in the course of another crime—most commonly robbery, burglary, or rape." Tucker states that the murder rate in the United States supports the theory of deterrence. The rate was low for the first six decades of the twentieth century, when the death penalty was swiftly applied. However, when states began to place a moratorium on the death penalty in 1966, followed by a Supreme Court decision that banned capital punishment for five years, the murder rate soared. A study by Karl Spence, a researcher at Texas A&M University, supports Tucker's argument. According to Spence, there were fifty-six executions in America and 9,140 murders in 1960. Nine years later, there were no executions and 14,590 murders. By 1975, four years into the national ban on capital punishment, 20,510 murders occurred. By contrast, fifty-six criminals were executed in 1995 and the murder rate fell by 12 percent.

Death penalty proponents also assert that many foreign countries were safer before they abolished capital punishment. Wesley Lowe, who maintains a "Pro Death Penalty Page" on the World Wide Web, writes, "Since England abolished capital punishment [in 1971], the murder rate has subsequently doubled there and 75 English citizens have been murdered by released killers!" He also states that instituting the death penalty would benefit crime-ridden nations such as South Africa. Lowe argues that the behavior of rapists in that nation—they rape children instead of women out of fear of acquiring the AIDS virus—indicates that these criminals recognize that their actions can have lethal consequences, thus proving the deterrent effects of a death penalty. Dudley Sharp, the director of resources for the pro–death penalty organization Justice for All, also claims that the death penalty can lead to a decrease in capital crimes. He cites Saudi Arabia as a nation with "swift and sure executions and very low violent crime rates," though he adds that such a criminal justice system would not be popular in America.

While the deterrent effects of the death penalty may never be proven conclusively, the cartoonists in the following chapter present their opinions on how capital punishment can affect the behavior of prospective criminals.

Examining Cartoon 1:

"It Doesn't Decrease the Number of Murders..."

About the Cartoon

Dan Wasserman presents the claim that executing convicted killers does not reduce the number of murders in the United States. Instead, when the number of people executed—eighty-five in 2000—is added to the number of homicides, the result is an increase in total killings.

About the Cartoonist

In addition to his job as editorial cartoonist for the *Boston Globe*, Dan Wasserman has published *We've Been Framed*, a collection of cartoons about the Reagan presidency. His cartoons have also been published in *Time* and other national magazines.

Examining Cartoon 2:
"It'll Sure Cut Down on Repeat Offenders..."

About the Cartoon

Death penalty proponents assert that capital punishment deters crime in two ways. First, capital punishment is a "general deterrent" because executing a murderer sends the message to would-be murderers that committing a capital crime has deadly consequences. In addition, putting a murderer to death prevents that criminal from killing again and thus serves as a "specific deterrent." In this cartoon, Steve Kelley illustrates that while the death penalty's general deterrent effect can be debated, its effectiveness as a specific deterrent is without question.

About the Cartoonist

Steve Kelley is the former editorial cartoonist for the *San Diego Union-Tribune*. Among his honors was a first-place award in the National Headliner Awards.

Examining Cartoon 3:
"Good Idea, but We'd Get the Death Penalty."

About the Cartoon

By using sarcasm, Signe Wilkinson suggests in this cartoon that the death penalty will not deter teenagers or adults from committing violent crimes. The words spoken by the three adolescents are intended to illustrate the thought process that would presumably have to take place if capital punishment effectively deterred murder. As expressed here, this thinking appears ridiculous, indicating that the artist considers the theory of deterrence absurd.

About the Cartoonist

Wilkinson, who won the Pulitzer Prize for editorial cartooning in 1992, is the editorial cartoonist for the *Philadelphia Daily News* and a former president of the Association of American Editorial Cartoonists.

Chapter 3

The Fairness of the Death Penalty

Preface

On June 6, 2001, the U.S. Justice Department released a report stating there is no significant racial disparity in the application of the death penalty. According to the department, "The . . . data provides no evidence that minority defendants are subjected to bias or otherwise disfavored in decisions concerning capital punishment." The report found that between 1995 and 2000, the attorney general (who reviews potential death penalty cases submitted by federal prosecutors) sought the death penalty for 17 percent (71 out of 408) of African American defendants in potential capital cases, 9 percent (32 out of 350) of Hispanic defendants, and 27 percent (44 out of 166) of white defendants.

The American Civil Liberties Union questioned the department's findings, noting that the conclusions in the final report were considerably different from a preliminary report released in September 2000. In the earlier report, the Justice Department had found that in three out of every four cases in which a federal prosecutor sought the death penalty between 1995 and 2000, the defendant was a minority, with more than half of those cases involving an African American defendant. Because African Americans are 12 percent of the general population, they are disproportionately affected by such prosecutorial actions.

Critics of capital punishment also assert that minority defendants with white victims are more likely to get the death penalty than white defendants with African American victims. In its report "Executing Minorities—An American Tradition," the National Coalition Against the Death Penalty writes: "Nearly 90% of persons executed were convicted of killing whites, although people of color make up over half of all homicide victims in the United States."

A December 1995 article in *Issues and Controversies On File* states that between 1976 and late 1995, four white people were executed for killing African Americans, while ninety-six African Americans were put to death for murdering whites.

Death penalty advocates assert that if racial disparities exist, they are not an indication that capital punishment is unfair but rather that it should be applied more consistently. Legal scholar Ernest van den Haag has argued: "If and when discrimination occurs it should be corrected. Not, however, by letting the guilty blacks escape the death penalty because guilty whites do, but by making sure that the guilty white offenders suffer it as the guilty blacks do."

Others challenge the existence of racial disparities in death penalty cases. A study by the Rand Corporation concludes that white defendants who have been convicted of murder are sentenced to death more frequently than their minority counterparts. According to the study, 32 percent of convicted white defendants in capital cases are sentenced to death, compared to 27 percent of convicted nonwhite defendants. The study also argues that any disparity between the treatment of murderers of white victims and minority victims is due to variables such as the severity of the crime and the number of crimes committed.

Minorities are not the only group whose treatment by the American death penalty system has been investigated; other groups include juveniles and the mentally disabled. The cartoonists in the following chapter present their views on the fairness of capital punishment.

Examining Cartoon 1:
"From Our Vantage Point . . ."

About the Cartoon

In this cartoon, Kirk Anderson presents one of the major arguments against the death penalty: that it is imposed disproportionately on African Americans and Hispanics. In a report issued by the Justice Department on June 6, 2001, Attorney General John Ashcroft stated that white defendants are more likely to be subjected to the death penalty. That report refuted the preliminary findings released by the department in September 2000. The earlier report had stated that the defendant was a minority in 75 percent of the cases in which a federal prosecutor had sought the death penalty since 1995. In over 50 percent of those cases, the defendant was an African American. Anderson suggests that in order to reach the conclusion that whites are more likely to be subject to the death penalty, the facts must be turned upside down.

About the Cartoonist

Kirk Anderson has been the editorial cartoonist for the *St. Paul Pioneer Press* since 1995. His cartoons have also appeared in hundreds of magazines, newspapers, and books, most notably the *New York Times, Los Angeles Times,* and *Washington Post.* Anderson also teaches editorial cartooning to a variety of individuals and groups.

Examining Cartoon 2:
"You Can Still Act Like the Big Boys"

About the Cartoon

Since 1976, eighteen people have been executed for crimes committed as teenagers. In this cartoon, Gary Markstein comments on the Supreme Court's June 1989 ruling that executing prisoners who were at least sixteen years old when they committed a capital crime does not violate the Eighth Amendment of the Constitution, which forbids "cruel and unusual punishment." Of the thirty-eight states with the death penalty, twenty-three have set a minimum age for death penalty sentences under eighteen. According to Markstein's argument, sixteen- and seventeen-year-olds who choose to commit serious crimes ought to realize they will not be treated like children.

About the Cartoonist

Gary Markstein is an editorial cartoonist for the *Milwaukee Journal-Sentinel.* In 2000 he received a first-place award from Global Media. Markstein also finished first in the 1997 Fischetti Editorial Cartoon competition.

Examining Cartoon 3:
"We'll Notify You Electronically"

About the Cartoon

One long-standing controversy concerning the death penalty, as shown in this cartoon by Steve Sack, is whether it is fair to execute the mentally incompetent. Since 1976, when the United States reinstated the death penalty, at least thirty-three mentally retarded (having an IQ under 70) men have been executed. The Supreme Court ruled in a 5-4 vote in 1989 that executing someone with a low IQ does not constitute "cruel and unusual punishment." (In March 2001, the Court agreed to reconsider the argument the following fall; a decision had not been announced by the time this book went to press.) Despite the 1989 ruling, seventeen of the thirty-eight states that use capital punishment have banned the executions of the mentally retarded.

Sack depicts a darkly humorous scenario in this cartoon. If the Supreme Court decides to set a minimum IQ for criminals on death row, then prisoners who score high enough will be "notified electronically"—in other words, face execution, most likely in an electric chair. Such a decision, if it is made, could affect the future of numerous death row inmates. Experts believe that between 10 and 15 percent of death row inmates are mentally retarded.

About the Cartoonist

Steve Sack is a nationally syndicated cartoonist and the editorial cartoonist for the *Minneapolis Star-Tribune*.

Chapter 4

The Death Penalty and the Legal System

Preface

C ritics of the death penalty often question whether the legal system has sufficient safeguards to ensure that no innocent person faces execution. They charge that this situation occurs frequently, pointing to examples such as Anthony Porter, who escaped execution in Illinois when a Northwestern University journalism professor and five of his students proved that another man had committed the murders for which Porter had been convicted. The debate over wrongful convictions also focuses on whether death penalty moratoriums should be established so that these convictions do not lead to the execution of innocent prisoners.

Some studies suggest the legal system is not infallible. Columbia Law School professor James S. Liebman's study, *A Broken System: Error Rates in Capital Cases, 1973–1995*, found such serious errors in 68 percent of death penalty cases that the death sentence or conviction was overturned. The reversals of sentences and verdicts can be a lengthy process and are often limited by laws that restrict reviews of death penalty cases.

The growing awareness of these errors has led to steps to prevent wrongful executions. In January 2000, in response to the release of Porter and the exoneration of twelve other death-row inmates since 1977, Illinois governor George Ryan declared a moratorium on executions in his state, stating, "I cannot support a system which, in its administration, has proven so fraught with error." The moratorium was prompted in part by a *Chicago Tribune* report, which revealed that "fundamental error" had led to the reversal of more than one-third of the 285 capital convictions in the state since 1977. In addition to the moratorium, Ryan established the Commission on Capital Punishment to investigate why Illinois has so many false convictions.

Illinois is not the only state to reconsider capital punishment. A dozen states considered moratorium or abolition legislation in 2000. Nebraska's legislature passed a moratorium in 1999, but the governor vetoed it. A bill in New Hampshire to abolish the death penalty met with a similar fate, while a moratorium bill died in the Maryland senate. Despite the legislative setbacks, interest in a nationwide moratorium is strong. A poll conducted by NBC and the *Wall Street Journal* in July 2000 revealed that 63 percent of Americans support a moratorium in order to determine whether the death sentence is applied fairly.

The theory that innocent defendants are frequently convicted has met with sharp criticism from death penalty advocates. Dudley Sharp, the director of resources for the pro–death penalty organization Justice for All, asserts that the guilt accuracy rate for death row inmates is 99.4 percent. Responding to a July 1997 report by the Death Penalty Information Center, an organization that opposes capital punishment, Sharp states: "Opponents claim that 69 'innocent' death row inmates have been released since 1973. Just a casual review, using the DPIC's own case descriptions, reveals that of 39 cases reviewed, that the DPIC offers no evidence of innocence in 29, or 78%, of those cases."

Death penalty advocates also argue that moratoriums are not necessary and could have deleterious effects. When asked whether he believes a moratorium is needed because of possible unfairness in the application of the death penalty, President George W. Bush declared: "I was the Governor of a State that had a death penalty, and as far as I was concerned, I reviewed every case, and I was confident that every person that had been put to death received full rights and was guilty of the crime." According to capital punishment supporters, even a brief moratorium could greatly affect America's crime rate. University of Houston–Clear Lake finance professors Roberto Marchesini and Dale Cloninger examined the effects of a temporary moratorium in Texas. The Texas Court of Criminal Appeals granted a stay of execution that lasted from January 2 to December 18, 1996, which led to the delay of all but three executions that year. Executions resumed on February 10, 1997. The professors reported that the moratorium resulted in

150 more murders during those thirteen months than would have been expected based on normal homicide rates.

The debate on wrongful convictions and moratoriums on the death penalty is part of a larger question: whether the legal system protects prisoners on death row or is too lenient. The cartoonists in the following chapters present their views on the death penalty and the legal system.

Examining Cartoon 1:
"Free a Death Row Inmate!"

About the Cartoon

Anthony Porter had been on Illinois's death row since 1983 for the murder of two Chicago teenagers, although he had long proclaimed that he was not guilty. He was two days away from being executed in February 1999 when a journalism professor at Northwestern University and five of his undergraduate students helped prove his innocence, leading to Porter's release from jail. Professor David Protess and his students, with the help of a private investigator, had uncovered evidence that led to the real culprit. Three years earlier, Protess and five students had helped free the wrongfully imprisoned "Ford Heights Four," four men who had been jailed—two placed on death row—for allegedly committing rape and murder. In this cartoon, Bolling mocks the ineffectiveness of many defense attorneys by exaggerating the youthfulness of the students who helped free Anthony Porter and suggesting that proving the innocence of a wrongfully convicted death row inmate is literally child's play.

About the Cartoonist

Ruben Bolling has drawn *Tom the Dancing Bug* since 1987; it was picked up by Universal Press Syndicate ten years later. The cartoon appears in the *Village Voice* and other alternative newspapers, along with daily publications such as the *Washington Post* and *San Jose Mercury-News*. Bolling has published two compilations, *All I Ever Needed to Know I Learned From My Golf-Playing Cats* and *Tom the Dancing Bug*.

Examining Cartoon 2:
"Death Penalty Debate"

About the Cartoon

Chuck Asay responds to several arguments against the death penalty in this cartoon. In the first two panels, he responds to the argument that innocent people have been executed by countering that even more people have been killed by murderers who have been allowed to go on living. In the third and fourth panels, Asay argues that the death penalty is widely supported in the United States, even though it might be unpopular in the rest of the world. In the fifth and sixth panels, the cartoonist rejects the claim that the death penalty is not a deterrent to murder by pointing out that it is seldom used. By depicting an overcrowded prison, Asay implies that executing prisoners would more effectively deter crime than simply warehousing them. In the final two panels, Asay rebuts the charge that the death penalty costs too much money by suggesting that the excessive costs are the result of delays and appeals generated by defendants and their lawyers.

About the Cartoonist

Chuck Asay is the editorial cartoonist for the *Colorado Springs Gazette* and is syndicated with Creators Syndicate in more than eighty newspapers nationwide. His collection of cartoons, *Asay Doodles Goes to Town*, was published in 1995.

Examining Cartoon 3:
"Green Mile Marathon"

About the Cartoon

In this cartoon, Doug MacGregor presents the byzantine legal process for death row inmates. ("Green mile" was a euphemism for death row in one of Stephen King's stories.) He suggests that the system is bogged down by too many appeals and reviews and that it should be simplified. Legal procedures resulted in an average stay on death row of eight years between 1973 and 1994, and the typical death penalty case costs $2 million dollars to litigate. However, limits on the number of appeals an inmate can file do exist, and the Supreme Court has restricted claims under the rule of habeas corpus to prove that a person has been unlawfully imprisoned. Such claims are filed if it is believed that the conviction was based on illegally obtained evidence, the defendant had ineffective counsel, or the jury was wrongfully chosen and impaneled.

About the Cartoonist

Doug MacGregor has been the editorial cartoonist for the *Fort Myers News-Press* in Florida since 1988 and is an eight-time Best-of-Gannett award winner. MacGregor has also received the Florida Press Club award twice.

Organizations to Contact

The editors have compiled the following list of organizations concerned with the issues debated in this book. The descriptions are derived from materials provided by the organizations. All have publications or information available for interested readers. The list was compiled on the date of publication of the present volume; the information provided here may change. Be aware that many organizations take several weeks or longer to respond to inquiries, so allow as much time as possible.

American Civil Liberties Union (ACLU)
Capital Punishment Project
125 Broad St., 18th Fl., New York, NY 10004
(212) 549-2500 • fax: (212) 549-2646
website: www.aclu.org

The project is dedicated to abolishing the death penalty. The ACLU believes that capital punishment violates the Constitution's ban on cruel and unusual punishment as well as the requirements of due process and equal protection under the law. It publishes and distributes numerous books and pamphlets, including "The Case Against the Death Penalty" and "Frequently Asked Questions Concerning the Writ of Habeas Corpus and the Death Penalty."

Amnesty International USA (AI)
322 Eighth Ave., New York, NY 10001
(212) 807-8400 • fax: (212) 627-1451
website: www.amnesty-usa.org

Amnesty International is an independent worldwide movement working impartially for the release of all prisoners of conscience, fair and prompt trials for political prisoners, and an end to torture and executions. AI is funded by donations from its members and supporters throughout the world. AI has published several books and reports, including *Fatal Flaws: Innocence and the Death Penalty*.

Canadian Coalition Against the Death Penalty (CCADP)

PO Box 38104, 550 Eglinton Ave. W, Toronto
ON M5N 3A8 Canada
(416) 693-9112 • fax: (416) 686-1630
e-mail: ccadp@home.com • website: www.ccadp.org

CCADP is a not-for-profit international human rights organization dedicated to educating the public on alternatives to the death penalty worldwide and to providing emotional and practical support to death row inmates, their families, and the families of murder victims. The coalition releases pamphlets and periodic press releases, and its website includes a student resource center providing research information on capital punishment.

Death Penalty Focus of California

74 New Montgomery, Suite 250, San Francisco, CA 94105
(415) 243-0143 • fax: (415) 243-0994
e-mail: info@deathpenalty.org • website: www.deathpenalty.org

Death Penalty Focus of California is a nonprofit organization dedicated to the abolition of capital punishment through grassroots organization, research, and the dissemination of information about the death penalty and its alternatives. It publishes the quarterly newsletter *The Sentry*.

Death Penalty Information Center (DPIC)

1606 20th St. NW, 2nd Fl., Washington, DC 20009
(202) 347-2531
website: www.essential.org/dpic

DPIC conducts research into public opinion on the death penalty. The center believes capital punishment is discriminatory and excessively costly and that it may result in the execution of innocent persons. It publishes numerous reports, such as "Millions Misspent: What Politicians Don't Say About the High Costs of the Death Penalty," "Innocence and the Death Penalty: Assessing the Danger of Mistaken Executions," and "With Justice for Few: The Growing Crisis in Death Penalty Representation."

Justice Fellowship

PO Box 16069, Washington, DC 20041-6069
(703) 904-7312 • fax: (703) 478-9679
website: www.justicefellowship.org

This Christian organization bases its work for reform of the justice system on the concept of victim-offender reconciliation. It does not take a position on the death penalty, but it publishes the pamphlet "Capital Punishment: A Call to Dialogue."

Justice for All

PO Box 55159, Houston, TX 77255
(713) 935-9300 • fax: (713) 935-9301
e-mail: jfanet@msn.com • website: www.jfa.net

Justice for All is a not-for-profit criminal justice reform organization that supports the death penalty. Its activities include circulating online petitions to keep violent offenders from being paroled early and publishing the monthly newsletter *The Voice of Justice*.

Justice Now

PO Box 62132, North Charleston, SC 29419-2132
e-mail: ranlerch@geocities.com
website: www.geocities.com/CapitolHill/8169

This organization supports the death penalty as a solution to the problems of crime and overcrowded prisons in the United States. It maintains information resources, which are available to the public, consisting of books, pamphlets, periodicals, newspaper clippings, and bibliographies about serial killers, death row prisoners, executions, prisons, and courts.

Lamp of Hope Project

PO Box 305, League City, TX 77574-0305
e-mail: ksebung@c-com.net • website: www.lampofhope.org

The project was extablished and is run primarily by Texas death row inmates. It works for victim-offender reconciliation and for the protection of the civil rights of prisoners, particularly the right of habeas corpus appeal. It publishes and distributes the periodical *Texas Death Row Journal.*

Lincoln Institute for Research and Education
1001 Connecticut Ave. NW, Washington, DC 20036
(202) 223-5112

The institute is a conservative think tank that studies public policy issues affecting the lives of black Americans, including the issue of the death penalty, which it favors. It publishes the quarterly *Lincoln Review.*

National Coalition to Abolish the Death Penalty (NCADP)
1436 U St. NW, Suite 104, Washington, DC 20009
(202) 387-3890 • fax: (202) 387- 5590
e-mail: info@ncadp • website: www.ncadp.org

The NCADP is a collection of more than 115 groups working together to stop executions in the United States. The organization compiles statistics on the death penalty. To further its goal, the coalition publishes *Legislative Action to Abolish the Death Penalty*, information packets, pamphlets, and research materials.

National Criminal Justice Reference Service (NCJRS)
U.S. Department of Justice
PO Box 6000, Rockville, MD 20849-6000
(301) 519-5500 • (800) 851-3420
e-mail: askncjrs@ncjrs.org • website: www.ncjrs.org

The National Criminal Justice Reference Service is one of the most extensive sources of information on criminal and juvenile justice in the world. For a nominal fee, this clearinghouse provides topical searches and reading lists on many areas of criminal justice, including the death penalty. It publishes an annual report on capital punishment.

For Further Research

Books

James R. Acker, Robert M. Bohm, and Charles S. Lanier, eds., *America's Experiment with Capital Punishment: Reflections on the Past, Present, and Future of the Ultimate Penal Sanction*. Durham, NC: Carolina Academic Press, 1998.

Amnesty International, *United States of America, Failing the Future: Death Penalty Developments, March 1998–March 2000*. New York: Amnesty International, 2000.

Hugo Adam Bedau, ed., *The Death Penalty in America*. New York: Oxford University Press, 1997.

John D. Bessler, *Death in the Dark: Midnight Executions in America*. Boston: Northeastern University Press, 1997.

Antoinette Bosco, *Choosing Mercy: A Mother of Murder Victims Pleads to End the Death Penalty*. Maryknoll, NY: Orbis Books, 2001.

Mark Costanzo, *Just Revenge: Costs and Consequences of the Death Penalty*. New York: St. Martin's Press, 1997.

Ted Gottfried, *Capital Punishment: The Death Penalty Debate*. Springfield, NJ: Enslow, 1997.

Harry Henderson, ed., *Capital Punishment*. New York: Facts On File, 2000.

Burt Henson and Ross R. Olney, *Furman v. Georgia: The Death Penalty and the Constitution*. New York: Franklin Watts, 1996.

Robert Jay Lifton and Greg Mitchell, *Who Owns Death?: Capital Punishment, the American Conscience, and the End of Executions*. New York: Morrow, 2000.

Dan Malone, *America's Condemned: Death Row Inmates in Their Own Words*. Kansas City: Andrews McMeel, 1999.

Gary E. McCuen, ed., *The Death Penalty and the Disadvantaged*. Hudson, WI: GEM, 1997.

Michael Mello, *Dead Wrong: A Death Row Lawyer Speaks Out Against Capital Punishment*. Madison: University of Wisconsin Press, 1997.

———, *The Wrong Man: A True Story of Innocence on Death Row*. Minneapolis: University of Minnesota Press, 2001.

Lane Nelson and Burk Foster, *Death Watch: A Death Penalty Anthology*. Upper Saddle River, NJ: Prentice-Hall, 2001.

Kathleen A. O'Shea and Ann Patrick Conrad, *Women and the Death Penalty in the United States, 1900–1998*. Westport, CT: Praeger, 1999.

Louis J. Palmer, *Encyclopedia of Capital Punishment in the United States*. Jefferson, NC: McFarland, 2001.

Louis P. Pojman and Jeffrey Reiman, *The Death Penalty: For and Against*. Lanham, MD: Rowman & Littlefield, 1998.

Austin Sarat, *When the State Kills: Capital Punishment and the American Condition*. Princeton, NJ: Princeton University Press, 2001.

Glen H. Stassen, ed., *Capital Punishment: A Reader*. Cleveland: Pilgrim Press, 1998.

Lloyd Steffen, *Executing Justice: The Moral Meaning of the Death Penalty*. Cleveland: Pilgrim Press, 1998.

Ted R. Weiland, *Capital Punishment: Deterrent or Catalyst*. Eugene, OR: Far Horizons Press, 2000.

Periodicals

Craig Aaron, "Criminal Injustice System," *In These Times*, December 27, 1998.

America, "Death Penalty Moratoriums," March 18, 2000.

Alan Berlow, "The Broken Machinery of Death," *American Prospect*, July 30, 2001.

Raymond Bonner, "Drawing a Line on Death," *New York Times*, June 24, 2001.

William F. Buckley Jr., "Miss Tucker's Plea," *National Review*, March 9, 1998.

Fox Butterfield, "Ambivalence? Incompetence? Fairness?: Behind the Death Row Bottleneck," *New York Times*, December 25, 1998.

————, "New Study Adds to Evidence of Bias in Death Sentences," *New York Times*, June 7, 1998.

Commonweal, "We, the Jury: But Not in Capital Cases," June 2, 2000.

Clay S. Conrad, "'Death-Qualification' Leads to Biased Juries," *USA Today*, March 2001.

Tom Flynn, "Of Malice and Mercy," *Free Inquiry*, Summer 2001.

David Gelernter, "What Do Murderers Deserve?" *Commentary*, April 1998.

Judy Gross, "Executions Continue; So Does Debate," *National Catholic Reporter*, February 20, 1998. Available from 115 East Armour Blvd., Kansas City, MO 64111.

Harper's, "The Executioner's Song and Dance," August 2001.

Bob Herbert, "Death-Penalty Dissenters," *New York Times*, July 9, 2001.

Issues and Controversies On File, "Death Penalty," May 1, 1998. Available from Facts On File News Services, 11 Penn Plaza, New York, NY 10001-2006.

Claudia Kolker, "Death Penalty Moratorium Idea Attracts Even Conservatives," *Los Angeles Times*, August 29, 2000.

Thomas K. Lowenstein, "Against Execution," *American Prospect*, August 28, 2000.

Will Manning and Jacqueline Rhoden-Trader, "Rethinking the Death Penalty," *Corrections Today*, October 2000.

John McCormick, "The Wrongly Condemned," *Newsweek*, November 9, 1998.

John O'Sullivan, "A Logical and Just Practice," *National Review*, July 17, 2000.

William Saletan, "Calculating the Risk," *Mother Jones*, July 2000.

Raymond A. Schroth, "Sister Helen Prejean: On Death Row," *Commonweal*, October 6, 2000.

Bruce Shapiro, "Dead Reckoning," *Nation*, August 6, 2001.

William Tucker, "The Chair Deters," *National Review*, July 17, 2000.

Ernest van den Haag, "The Ultimate Penalty . . . and a Just One: The Basics of Capital Punishment," *National Review*, June 11, 2001.

Wall Street Journal, "Gender and Death," February 2, 1998.

James Q. Wilson, "Executing the Retarded," *National Review*, July 23, 2001.

——, "What Death-Penalty Errors?" *New York Times*, July 10, 2000.

Index